MINDFUL COOKING

BY STEPHANIE FINNE

BLUE OWL BOOKS

TIPS FOR CAREGIVERS

Social and emotional learning (SEL) helps children manage emotions, create and achieve goals, maintain relationships, learn how to feel empathy, and make good decisions. The SEL approach will help children establish positive habits in communication, cooperation, and decision-making. By incorporating SEL in early reading, children will be better equipped to build confidence and foster positive peer networks.

BEFORE READING

Talk to the reader about kitchen safety.

Discuss: What can happen if you don't take your time in the kitchen? What can you do to lessen distractions? How does that relate to mindfulness?

AFTER READING

Talk to the reader about how mindful cooking can help him or her focus.

Discuss: Cooking takes concentration. How does cooking help you focus on your senses? What part of cooking feels the most creative to you?

SEL GOAL

Some students may struggle with self-awareness, making it hard to regulate their emotions, thoughts, and behaviors. Mindful cooking can help readers develop these skills by learning to slow down and focus. This can help them manage stress and control impulses in other areas of their lives.

TABLE OF CONTENTS

CHAPTER 1

WHAT IS MINDFUL COOKING?

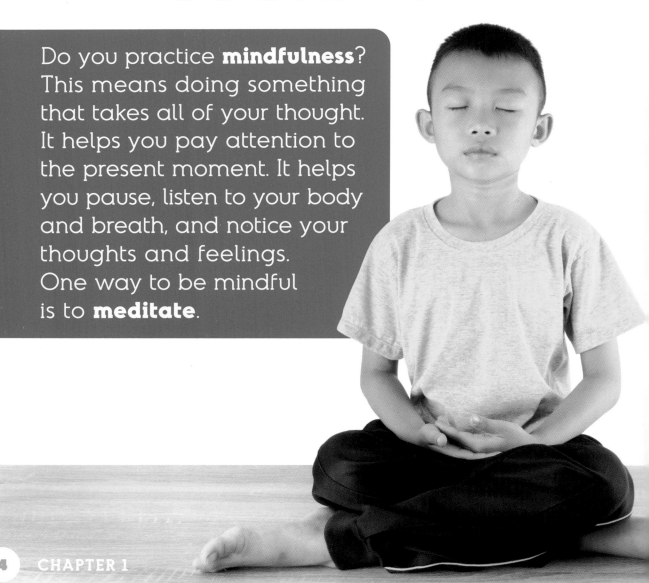

Do you practice **mindfulness**? This means doing something that takes all of your thought. It helps you pay attention to the present moment. It helps you pause, listen to your body and breath, and notice your thoughts and feelings. One way to be mindful is to **meditate**.

Another way is by being creative. This includes cooking! When cooking, it is important to slow down and follow a **recipe**. This helps us **focus** and be mindful.

CHAPTER 2

MINDFUL FOOD PREP

All parts of cooking can be done mindfully. The first step is to set your **intention**. Are you cooking to be creative or to feed your family? Maybe you are doing both! Then choose a recipe. Be mindful of the meal you choose. Pick foods that **nourish** your body and mind.

Then, make a list of the **ingredients**. While shopping, take time to examine each item. How does it look and smell? What flavor will it add to your dish?

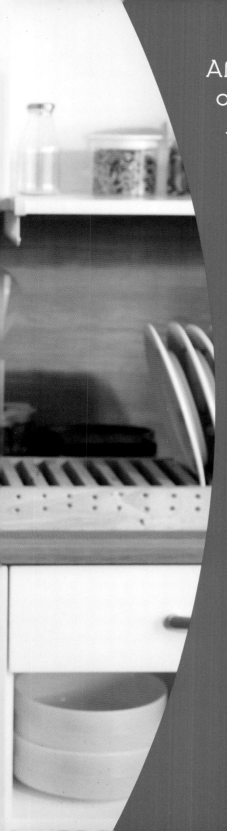

After shopping, read the recipe again and gather your supplies. As you move around the kitchen, focus on your body's movements. Are you moving fast or slow? Is your body **tense** or relaxed? Noticing how your body is moving and how your heart is beating can help you be present and focus on what you are doing.

BE PRESENT

Be present in your body and mind as you cook. Try to forget any worries. Think of one thing you are **grateful** for, such as your nose to smell or your teeth to chew the food you are preparing.

Begin following the recipe. Always check with an adult before using knives or a stove or oven. Why? Staying safe is part of being mindful. Focus on each step. When chopping, move slowly.

HELPFUL HINT: Tuck your fingers when chopping.

CHAPTER 3

LET'S COOK!

Let's focus on cooking homemade personal pizzas! Here's what you need:

RECIPES

Ingredients:
- 14 to 16 ounces premade pizza dough
- 1 to 2 cups pizza sauce
- 4 to 6 ounces shredded cheese
- your favorite toppings

Supplies:
- 2 baking sheets
- parchment paper
- cutting board
- knife
- bowls
- rolling pin
- spoon
- hot pads

Step 1: Ask an adult to preheat the oven to 400 degrees Fahrenheit (205 degrees Celsius). Cut parchment paper to fit on the baking sheets.

Step 2: Prepare the toppings. Focus on chopping each vegetable. Put each topping in a bowl. Think about where each ingredient came from. Notice their smells and **textures**.

HELPFUL HINT: If you need more than four pizzas, double your recipe.

Step 3: Carefully split the dough into four equal sections. Roll, stretch, or press each section into a 6- to 8-inch (15- to 20-centimeter) round. Take time to feel the dough in your fingers. What words would you use to describe how it feels? Place two rounds on top of the parchment paper on each baking sheet.

Step 4: Add 2 to 3 spoonfuls of pizza sauce to each round. Use the spoon to spread the sauce on the dough.

Step 5: Be creative with your toppings! Make a face or fun design.

Step 6: Ask an adult to put the pizzas in the oven. Bake for 8 minutes. Then turn the baking sheet and bake for an additional 5 to 10 minutes, checking on them every couple of minutes. As the pizzas bake, **reflect** on the cooking **process**.

Step 7: Have an adult remove the pizzas from the oven using hot pads. Let the pizzas cool before cutting. Practice mindful breathing while you wait. Breathe in the smell of the pizza.

Step 8: Eat and enjoy! Think about the food you just made. How does it smell, look, and taste?

MINDFUL EATING

Turn off all distractions. Show gratitude for the work it took to make the meal. Take time to enjoy each bite.

Step 9: The last part of mindful cooking is cleanup. While cleaning, think about the meal. Did everything taste like you thought it would? How did cooking with focus make you feel?

LEARNING FROM COOKING

Not all recipes turn out on the first try. That's OK! Reflect on what happened. Would you do anything differently next time? Cooking is all about learning!

HELPFUL HINT: Leaving the kitchen clean reduces **stress** and makes it easier to start cooking the next time.

GOALS AND TOOLS

GROW WITH GOALS

Being mindful in the kitchen can help you be present and help you focus. Try these things to cook mindfully.

Goal: Think about what you want to eat and why. Does a certain food sound good because it brings you comfort? Do you want to make a recipe because it looks challenging?

Goal: Show gratitude for the ingredients you are using. Think about what it took to get those ingredients to your kitchen. Be thankful for all the people who helped grow and produce the food you are about to eat.

Goal: Eat with intention. With each bite, pay attention to your senses. How does the sight, taste, smell, and feel of each bite influence your mood?

TRY THIS!

When eating, use all of your senses. This will help you mindfully experience your food. Try it with one of the main pizza toppings: cheese! Pick a piece of cheese. Take a few deep breaths. Then focus on each of your senses:

sight: What color is the cheese? Is it shredded or cubed?

touch: Is the cheese cold? Is it soft and squishy?

smell: How does the cheese smell? Is it different from the other ingredients?

sound: Does the cheese make sounds when you squish it gently by your ear?

taste: When the cheese is on your tongue, can you taste the flavors? Are there any flavors left after you chew and swallow?

GLOSSARY

focus
To concentrate on something.

grateful
Feeling or showing thanks.

ingredients
Items used to make something.

intention
Something you mean to do.

meditate
To think deeply and quietly as
a way of relaxing your mind
and body.

mindfulness
A mentality achieved by focusing
on the present moment and calmly
recognizing and accepting your
feelings, thoughts, and sensations.

nourish
To provide the substances necessary
for growth, health, and good condition.

process
A series of actions or steps that
create something.

recipe
A set of instructions for preparing food.

reflect
To think carefully or seriously
about something.

stress
Mental or emotional strain or pressure.

tense
Stretched stiff and tight, or unable
to relax.

textures
The ways things feel, especially
how rough or smooth they are.

TO LEARN MORE

FACT SURFER

Finding more information is as easy as 1, 2, 3.

1. Go to www.factsurfer.com

2. Enter "**mindfulcooking**" into the search box.

3. Choose your book to see a list of websites.

INDEX

Blue Owl Books are published by Jump!, 5357 Penn Avenue South, Minneapolis, MN 55419, www.jumplibrary.com

Copyright © 2022 Jump! International copyright reserved in all countries. No part of this book may be reproduced in any form without written permission from the publisher.

Library of Congress Cataloging-in-Publication Data

Names: Finne, Stephanie, author.
Title: Mindful cooking / by Stephanie Finne.
Description: Minneapolis: Jump!, Inc., 2022.
Series: The art of mindfulness
Includes index. | Audience: Ages 7–10
Identifiers: LCCN 2021030762 (print)
LCCN 2021030763 (ebook)
ISBN 9781636903583 (hardcover)
ISBN 9781636903590 (paperback)
ISBN 9781636903606 (ebook)
Subjects: LCSH: Cooking. | LCGFT: Cookbooks.
Classification: LCC TX714 F5646 2022 (print) | LCC TX714 (ebook) | DDC 641.5–dc23
LC record available at https://lccn.loc.gov/2021030762
LC ebook record available at https://lccn.loc.gov/2021030763

Editor: Jenna Gleisner
Designer: Michelle Sonnek

Photo Credits: Warut Chinsai/Shutterstock, cover; Max Topchii/Shutterstock, 1; thondonal88/Shutterstock, 3; Torychemistry/Shutterstock, 4; s_oleg/Shutterstock, 5; StockImageFactory.com/Shutterstock, 6; FG Trade/iStock, 7; Chachamp/Shutterstock, 8–9; PK Studio/Shutterstock, 10–11; Noel V. Baebler/Shutterstock, 12; Africa Studio/Shutterstock, 13; Alona Siniehina/Shutterstock, 14–15; Odua Images/Shutterstock, 16–17; arrowsmith2/Shutterstock, 18–19; pikselstock/Shutterstock, 20–21.

Printed in the United States of America at Corporate Graphics in North Mankato, Minnesota.